Francisco Coronado

Karen Price Hossell

Heinemann Library
Chicago, Illinois

Page layout and maps by 3 Loop 9, Los Angeles, CA
Photo research by Amor Montes de Oca
Printed and bound in the United States by Lake Book Manufacturing, Inc.

07 06 05 04 03
10 9 8 7 6 5 4 3 2 1

Library of Congress Cataloging-in-Publication Data
Price Hossell, Karen, 1957-
  Francisco Coronado / Karen Price Hossell.
      p. cm. -- (Groundbreakers)
Summary: A biography of the sixteenth-century Spanish explorer who
searched for cities of gold in parts of the American Southwest, but
found only Indian villages.
Includes bibliographical references and index.
  ISBN 1-4034-0242-6 (Lib. bdg.) -- ISBN 1-4034-0478-X (pbk.)
  1. Coronado, Francisco Vásquez de, 1510-1554--Juvenile literature.
2. Explorers--America--Biography--Juvenile literature. 3.
Explorers--Spain--Biography--Juvenile literature. 4. Southwest,
New--Discovery and exploration--Spanish--Juvenile literature. 5.
America--Discovery and exploration--Spanish--Juvenile literature. [1.
Coronado, Francisco Vásquez de, 1510-1554. 2. Explorers. 3. Southwest,
New--Discovery and exploration. 4. America--Discovery and
exploration--Spanish.] I. Title. II. Series.
  E125.V3 P74 2002
  979'.01'092--dc21

                                          2002008341

Acknowledgments
The author and publishers are grateful to the following for permission to reproduce copyright material:
p. 4 Collection of the Roswell Museum and Art Center, Peter Hurd, Portrait of Coronado, 1937-40
charcoal on paper, Gift of the Artist, 1955.023.001; pp. 5, 26, 27, 33, 40 John Elk III; pp. 6, 37 Robert
Frerck/Odyssey/Chicago; pp. 7, 12 Archivo Iconografico, S.A./Corbis; pp. 8, 11, 15 The Granger
Collection, New York; pp. 9, 10, 19, 35 North Wind Picture Archives; pp. 13, 17 Palace of the
Governors Museum of New Mexico; pp. 14, 36 Stock Montage, Inc.; p. 16 Doug Scott/Age Fotostock;
p. 18 Hulton Archive/Getty Images; p. 20 Walt Anderson/Visuals Unlimited; p. 21 Richard T.
Nowitz/Corbis; p. 22 Oldmaps.com; pp. 23, 32 Sun Valley Photography/Nativestock.com; p. 24 J.
Dennis/Trip; p. 25 Kunsthistorisches Museum,Kunstkammer, Vienna, Austria/Art Resource; p. 28 N.
Carter/North Wind Picture Archives; p. 29 Bettmann/Corbis; p. 30 Michael S. Lewis/Corbis; p. 31
Willard Clay; p. 34 Eliot Cohen; p. 38 Robert Holmes/Corbis; p. 39 Amor Montes De Oca; p. 41
Michael Snell

Cover photograph: the Collection of the Roswell Museum and Art Center, Peter Hurd, Portrait of
Coronado, 1937-40 charcoal on paper, Gift of the Artist, 1955.023.001

Every effort has been made to contact copyright holders of any material reproduced in this book. Any
omissions will be rectified in subsequent printings if notice is given to the publisher.

Some words are shown in bold, **like this.** You can find out
what they mean by looking in the glossary.

Contents

Who Was Francisco Coronado?

Francisco Vásquez de Coronado was a Spanish general, governor, **conquistador**, and explorer. He left Spain for Mexico in 1535 and became governor of the Mexican **province** of New Galicia. In 1540, he was appointed to command a huge **expedition.** With a large army of more than 1,300 people, Coronado traveled through the American Southwest, searching for legendary cities of gold. Sometimes he divided up the expedition, each group exploring a different area. Altogether, the expedition members traveled through present-day Arizona, New Mexico, California, Texas, Oklahoma, and Kansas. The group became the first Europeans to travel through the interior of the American continent from the West. They were also the first to see **bison** and Rocky Mountain sheep.

An ambitious expedition

The expedition was put together by Antonio de Mendoza, who was the **viceroy** of New Spain and one of Coronado's closest friends. Mendoza arranged the expedition after hearing amazing stories about great cities north of Mexico. In those cities, he was told, the buildings were five stories tall, and the people wore jewelry made of gold and precious stones.

Francisco Coronado was born in Spain and came to Mexico to stay in 1535.

Since Coronado and his army traveled through the American Southwest in the 16th century, roads have been built, opening it up to travelers and settlers.

When the Spanish had conquered Mexico in 1521, they had found silver and gold, and when they conquered Peru in 1536, they again found mines of gold and silver. The idea that to the north there were more mines of gold, silver, and maybe copper—not to mention precious stones—excited Mendoza. He wanted to get the credit for finding another land as rich as Peru or Mexico, and he sent Coronado and his men off with great hopes about what they would find.

Opening up the West

No European had seen the region traveled by Coronado—the present southwestern United States—until he turned his army to the north in 1540 in search of these great cities. Spanish explorers such as Hernando de Soto and Juan Ponce de Leon had explored the southeast, and other explorers had sailed along the coast. The members of the Coronado expedition, though, were the first to see the Great Plains and the Grand Canyon.

Francisco was born into a **noble** family in Salamanca, Spain, in about 1510. In Spain in the 1500s, the oldest son usually **inherited** most of the family's property and money. A small amount of money was then divided among the rest of the children. Francisco had an older brother, so he knew he would not inherit the family **estate.** Instead, he would have to find his own way in life.

Education

Because he came from a noble family, Francisco had many **privileges** while growing up. While little is known about his childhood, he was almost certainly well educated for that time. He would have studied mathematics, science, **philosophy**, and Latin, among other courses. Later, someone wrote that Coronado was always interested in "science." From the description that follows, however, it appears that the kind of science that fascinated Coronado is not considered science today. The kinds of sciences that Coronado enjoyed included magic and fortune-telling. Salamanca was home to a great **university,** the oldest in Spain. It is not known whether Coronado went to this university, although it was known for its courses in science.

Salamanca, Spain, where Coronado was born in about 1510, is about 130 miles (210 kilometers) from the capital, Madrid.

Spaniards were honored to be invited to attend events at the court of the king.

At court

Because Francisco was born into a noble family, he was welcome in the **court** of the king of Spain. This meant that when Francisco finished school, he was invited to parties, concerts, and other gatherings at the palace of the king. It was while at court that Coronado met Antonio de Mendoza, the man who was to help shape his future. Mendoza liked Coronado so much that he hired him to be his assistant. The king of Spain, Charles V, appointed Mendoza to be **viceroy** of New Spain in 1530, but Mendoza was unable to go to New Spain until 1535. Mendoza asked his young assistant to go with him, and the two men sailed together to the New World.

Coronado's Spain

One of the main reasons the people of Spain and their king wanted to explore the Americas was to find a water route to Asia. In the Middle Ages, Europe traded many goods, especially wool, for silk and spices from Asia. The route used to trade these products was called the Silk Road. Most **caravans** only traveled part of the way between Europe and China. They traded goods with other **merchants** along the way, in a sort of relay system.

For many years, the ruling Mongol tribe made sure the caravans could travel safely. In 1347, though, a terrible **plague** killed many Mongols. Another group of people called the Ottomans then began to move across Asia, taking over European trading posts and making travel unsafe. By 1470, the route was nearly closed, and Europeans began to search for a way to get to Asia by water. Traveling by boat would be faster and cheaper.

> *The Silk Road was actually a series of many different roads that linked Europe and China.*

The Spanish Empire

Spain was one of the countries determined to find the water route. It also wanted to expand its **empire** and its wealth. The king of Spain during Coronado's time was Charles V. Besides finding a way to reach Asia by water, Charles hoped that one of his explorers would find gold in the New World. When Hernán Cortés conquered Mexico in 1519 and found gold and silver mines, riches soon flowed into the Spanish **treasury,** and Cortes became a national hero.

Another goal of the empire was to **convert** the natives to Christianity. The official church of Spain was the Roman Catholic Church, and everyone in Spain was required to be a Catholic. The Spaniards thought that it was their responsibility to convert the people in the lands they conquered from their religion to Catholicism.

Charles V was the grandson of Queen Isabella and King Ferdinand, who funded the explorations of Christopher Columbus.

CLAIMING LAND FOR THE EMPIRE

Beginning in the 1400s, explorers from European countries such as Spain, England, and the Netherlands began to sail across the Atlantic and claim land for their own countries. There were several reasons why they believed they had the right to do this. One was because the people who lived in the lands they were claiming were not Christians. At that time, Christianity was the main religion in Europe, and Europeans believed that it was the one true religion. They felt that they were helping non-Christians by forcing them to follow Christianity. Europeans also believed that their culture was superior and that native peoples would benefit from learning European ways of life. Last, the Europeans saw new lands as an opportunity to become rich by exploiting the natural resources. The people who lived in the conquered lands were often unaware of the invader's reasons for taking over until it was too late.

The Spanish in Mexico

Spanish explorer Hernán Cortés invaded and conquered the **Aztec provinces** of Mexico in 1519. Cortes and about 400 Spanish **conquistadors** first came ashore at Veracruz. Then they marched inland, conquering settlements as they traveled. The Spaniards were impressed with what they saw. Many of the Aztec towns were orderly and well governed, similar to the towns back in Spain. What impressed the Spaniards even more was the amount of silver and gold in the land. Precious metals and gemstones were sold openly in the markets, and many Aztecs wore gold and silver jewelry. The Spaniards knew that this land would be an important addition to the Spanish **empire.**

The fall of Tenochtitlán

After capturing many small towns, Cortés and his soldiers conquered Tenochtitlán, the Aztec capital, in August 1521. During the battle, the Spaniards destroyed many buildings. After they removed the Aztec emperor from power, the Spaniards began to rebuild the city. They forced the Aztecs who remained there to work for them. The Spaniards wanted the new city to look like the cities in Spain, so they built a city hall and a large **plaza** in the shape of a rectangle. A palace was built for Cortés and the city was renamed Mexico City. By 1524, about 30,000 people lived there.

Hernán Cortés sailed to Mexico in 1519 with only 11 ships, 500 soldiers, and 13 horses. This small force conquered an empire.

The Aztecs were skilled at smelting gold. Smelting is a way of separating a metal from its ore.

New Spain

As they rebuilt Mexico City, the Spaniards established a **colony** in Mexico. Cities and towns were reorganized, and the natives who lived in them were required to pay taxes to the Spanish government. They were forced to turn away from their religion and to become Christians. Mexico became a part of New Spain, which was the name for all of Spain's **colonies** in the New World. It included all of present-day Mexico, along with parts of Central America, as well as Cuba and Peru. For several years, Spain sent leaders to New Spain, but they did not do a good job. In 1535, the Spanish government decided to send a **viceroy** to New Spain to rule the country. The king appointed Antonio de Mendoza as the first viceroy of New Spain. Because Coronado was Mendoza's assistant, he sailed across the Atlantic to New Spain with him.

THE AZTECS

The Aztecs had lived in present-day Mexico since the 13th century. The Spaniards were surprised to discover how advanced the Aztec civilization was. When they needed more farmland, the Aztecs made floating islands in lakes by piling dirt on top of rafts and planting crops on them. In the capital city of Tenochtitlán, they built canals and bridges. They built **dikes** to stop flooding in the city and huge, pyramid-like temples to their gods. They studied **astronomy,** mathematics, and medicine, among many other things.

Early Years in New Spain

In New Spain, Coronado worked hard and earned the respect of the people of Mexico City. At first he worked as an official inspector, and as he did that job he got to meet many government leaders. In 1537, he stopped a **rebellion** by African slaves who had been brought to Mexico. Because

THE DISCOVERY OF CHOCOLATE

Hernán Cortés may have become the first European to taste chocolate when he drank the frothy beverage at an **Aztec** banquet in 1519. The Aztecs thought the drink made a person wiser and stronger, and they allowed only priests and rulers to drink chocolate. According to one story, they served the drink in cups made from pure gold. Cortés thought the drink was very bitter, but he brought cacao beans to Spain. The Spanish sweetened the drink and served it at important meals at **court.** Eventually, the drink became popular throughout Europe.

Coronado was a good leader, **Viceroy** Mendoza made him the governor of a large **province** in northwest Mexico called New Galicia. While governor, he had roads built in New Galicia and made sure the people of the province were safe from attacks from native Mexicans who lived in the surrounding area.

*This map shows the **colony** of New Spain in 1579.*

Coronado marries

After he had been in Mexico for about three years, Coronado met and married Beatriz Estrada. When Coronado met Beatriz, her father was the treasurer of Mexico, in charge of all its finances. At one time, he had been the governor of Mexico, and he was a wealthy and respected man. Everyone who knew Beatriz spoke of what a kind woman she was and of how much she and Coronado loved each other. She and Coronado had at least five children. During his **expeditions,** Coronado missed them very much.

VICEROY ANTONIO DE MENDOZA

Antonio de Mendoza was born into a **noble** family in Granada, Spain, where his father, the Count of Tendilla, was the royal commander. Mendoza became a city councilman in Granada in 1513 and viceroy of New Spain in 1535. As viceroy, one of the first things Mendoza did was to ask the city leaders of Mexico City to straighten and widen the streets. He also requested that colonnades—covered walkways—be built around the city square so people would have shelter from rain. The same thing had been done in Granada. In Mexico City, Mendoza lived in a grand palace on the city's central **plaza.** With the help of New Spain's bishop, Mendoza also founded two schools to educate Aztecs in New Spain: the Colegio de Santa Cruz de Tlateloco and the Royal and Pontifical **University** of Mexico. In 1550, Mendoza was appointed viceroy of Peru. He died in 1552.

The Seven Cities of Gold

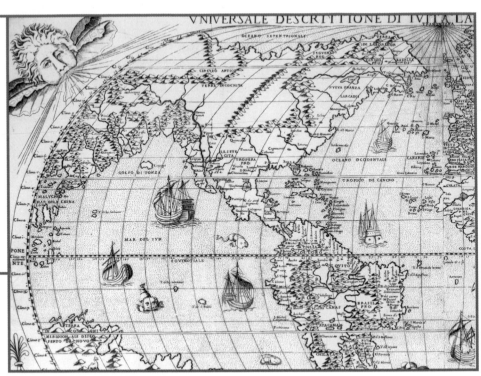

In Coronado's time, maps were not always accurate. This map of the world, made in 1565, shows North America connected to Asia. It also shows the Seven Cities of Gold, even though no one had found them.

For many years, stories were told among the peoples of the New World. They told of large cities to the north of Mexico. The buildings in the cities were tall for that time—four or five stories high—and the people who lived in them wore jewelry made of gold and precious stones.

The Spaniards who lived in Mexico listened to these stories, and many believed them. In Mexico they had already found silver and gold. They were sure that if the cities in the stories were real, they could conquer them, too. Cortés had become a hero when he conquered Mexico. Like Cortés, the person who led such an **expedition** would become famous all over the world.

Shipwreck survivors

In 1536, four men walked into Mexico. They were Alvar Núñez Cabeza de Vaca, Andres Dorantes de Caranca, Alonza del Castillo Maldonado, and a slave named Estevanico. The men had been walking for a long time. They were the only remaining survivors of an expedition that had begun in 1527, led by the Spanish explorer Panfilo de Narvaez.

ESTEVANICO

Estevanico was born in Morocco in about 1503. He was sold into slavery by Portuguese traders in 1520 or 1521. Reports that mention him, including one written by Mendoza, show him as an intelligent man who was good with people. During his travels with de Vaca, Estevanico had made friends with the Native Americans. On the journey, he carried a tent, sleeping robes, and four green pottery plates that he liked to eat from. He also had two greyhounds. Estevanico wore feathers on his arms and legs and bells on his ankles and carried a "medicine rattle" made from a gourd decorated with feathers. When the group met with people he knew, they stopped to make camp, and Estevanico spent hours dancing and drinking with the Indians. He angered the people of Hawikuh, though, and they killed him.

A failed expedition

The purpose of the expedition was to conquer Florida and set up a **colony** there, but they were shipwrecked. There were only four survivors out of the entire expedition. They were found by a group of Native Americans and forced to work as slaves. After six years the Spaniards escaped and walked hundreds of miles until they reached Mexico from the north, becoming the first Europeans to do so. There, they were relieved to be reunited with other Spaniards.

The Spaniards living in Mexico gave the men food, water, and a place to sleep, then asked them many questions. They especially wanted to know if the men had seen anything like the legendary great cities they had heard about. They listened closely to Cabeza de Vaca and decided that the places he described sounded much like the great cities they had heard of all of their lives. Then they took the men to Mexico City, where de Vaca met with **Viceroy** Mendoza and told him about the great cities to the north.

Mendoza Arranges an Expedition

Soon, the news that the men had seen the cities of gold spread throughout the city. The men actually never said they had seen cities of gold, but each time the story was passed along, something else was added to it. Before long, the "tall buildings" de Vaca had described were being talked about in the streets of Mexico City as buildings made of gold and precious stones.

Antonio de Mendoza wanted to find out for sure whether these cities really did exist, and where they were. He asked a priest, Father Marcos de Niza, to look for the cities. De Niza, often called Fray Marcos, set off on his journey on March 7, 1539. With Fray Marcos were three **friars** and the slave Estevanico.

Stories of Cibola

In September, Fray Marcos and the friars returned without Estevanico. They reported that the he had been killed by Native Americans who lived in the north. Fray Marcos said that they had first traveled north into Arizona. At a river now called the Little Colorado, they turned east, into present-day New Mexico. There, they saw in the distance a large city, with high buildings. When Fray Marcos asked the local people about it, they told

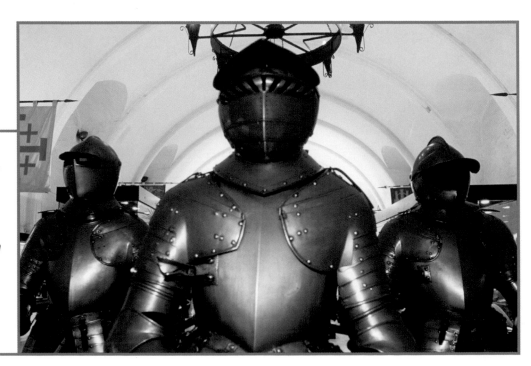

The strong metal armor used by the Spanish was an imporant advantage in their battles against the Native Americans.

him that the city was called Cibola. Fray Marcos and the other Spaniards did not visit the cities, but the natives told them that Cibola was one of seven such cities. Soon the people of Mexico were calling them the Seven Cities of Gold.

About 1,500 people went on the expedition, most of them on foot. Some of the Mexican natives brought along their entire families, including their wives and children.

Mendoza chooses Coronado

Mendoza quickly decided to arrange an **expedition** to find the cities. At first Mendoza himself wanted to lead the expedition. Then he realized that he should stay home to govern. He instead chose a man he trusted, a man he knew would do a good job: Francisco Vásquez de Coronado.

Preparing for the expedition

The news of the search for the Seven Cities of Gold spread quickly throughout Mexico. Before long, 300 Spaniards and 800 native Mexicans had volunteered to go along as members of the army. Coronado made sure that some of his friends and other people he trusted were included. To show how determined he was to be successful, he invested 50,000 **ducats** of his own money in the expedition. **Viceroy** Mendoza contributed 60,000 ducats. Altogether, the Spaniards spent what would be millions of dollars by today's standards on the expedition.

The Expedition Begins

You can follow Coronado's expedition on the map on pages 42–43.

The **expedition** was the largest one ever taken by Europeans in the New World. Besides an army of about 336 Spaniards on horseback, as many as 1,000 native Mexicans, along with their wives and children, went along as guides, cooks, **wranglers**, and foot soldiers.

Pedro de Castaneda, a member of the expedition who published his **memoirs** in 1565, said that about 1,000 horses and mules, 500 cows, and many rams and sheep accompanied the expedition. The army planned to use the animals, except for the horses, for food as they traveled. The explorers rode on some of the mules and horses and packed supplies on the rest. The soldiers carried swords and pulled cannon behind horses.

More supplies were put onto two ships. The ships were to sail from Mexico up the coast of Baja California. A few members of the expedition planned to meet the ships on the coast and collect supplies to carry back to the main army.

This painting showing Coronado's expedition is by Frederic Remington, who is famous for his paintings of the American West.

Departure

On February 22, 1540, everthing was ready. Coronado and his army gathered in Compostela, the capital of New Galicia. They were a magnificent sight. Coronado sat atop his horse at the head of the army of thousands. He wore golden armor that gleamed in the sunlight. His horse also wore armor. Behind Coronado were more than 300 soldiers on horseback. Many of them wore armor and carried **lances** and swords. At least 1,000 native Mexicans followed on foot. Many of the native Mexicans were **Aztecs** and Tarascans. They carried bows and arrows, clubs, and spears. Then came the animals, herded by more men on horseback.

Many Spanish explorers saw the conversion of the Indians to Christianity as their most important task. Most expeditions in the New World included several priests.

Mendoza's commands

Viceroy Mendoza came from Mexico City to see the expedition off. He gave Coronado several commands. First, he said, treat the native Mexicans who are acting as servants well. Then he said that when they reached Cibola and the other villages they would find on their journey, the army must not be cruel to the local people and should not take food or other supplies by force. Next, he said that the people of Cibola must promise to obey God and the king of Spain. Then Mendoza reminded the soldiers that they were expected to **convert** the people of the New World to Christianity. After a short religious service, the Spanish leaders swore their loyalty to Coronado. Then the huge band of explorers began their journey.

A Rough Journey

You can follow Coronado's expedition on the map on pages 42–43.

*The animals on the **expedition** had trouble walking across the hilly, rocky ground in northwestern Mexico.*

As they traveled, the explorers soon found that they had brought too many supplies. Because the land was rocky and uneven, the animals stumbled as they tried to walk on the rocks and through **gullies.** Poorly packed equipment slipped off horses, and the foot soldiers had to run back, pick things up, and put them back on the horses. Finally, they decided they would have to start leaving things behind. Many of the men had brought things they didn't need, such as extra items of clothing. Coronado most likely sent a messenger back to Compostela to ask his assistants to retrieve some of the discarded baggage. They also gave some of it away to people who lived in villages as they traveled through them.

At Chiametla, a group of Native Americans attacked the party. Coronado's closest military adviser, Lope de Samaniego, was shot and killed by an arrow shot through his eye. Angered, Coronado sent his soldiers to find the people who had attacked them. He then had them hanged.

Seeds of doubt

Before the main expedition had left, **Viceroy** Mendoza had ordered a small group of men, led by Melchior Diaz, to check out Fray Marcos's story about the cities of gold. The scouting party left in November 1539 and met up with Coronado's **expedition** after the incident at Chiametla. They brought bad news. The Native Americans they had spoken with on their journey all said that the stories of Cibola were untrue. There were six or seven villages that, as a group, were called Cibola. But the natives said that they were like any other **pueblo** village. The people of Cibola had some turquoise jewelry, but no metal at all, and certainly no gold. Diaz also said that the Native Americans would not be happy to see Coronado's army, and that they would fight for their land.

Coronado repeated the scouts' story to Fray Marcos. The priest said the natives were lying. They didn't want anyone else to find out about the great riches in Cibola, he said. Coronado chose to believe him. He and Mendoza, along with many others, had invested too much into the expedition to turn back after a few discouraging words.

The Native Americans of the Southwest are known for their beautiful turquoise jewelry, but Coronado was not impressed—he was more interested in gold.

Coronado and Fray Marcos Explore

YOU CAN FOLLOW CORONADO'S EXPEDITION ON THE MAP ON PAGES 42–43.

On March 28, 1540, the **expedition** moved on to Culiacan, where they planned to stay for the rest of the winter. Coronado decided that it would not be practical to send the entire army to look for Cibola, so he took a small band of men, including Fray Marcos, to search for the cities.

Coronado had brought sheep along on his scouting trip to kill and eat along the way. But the paths Coronado and his men traveled were hilly and full of rocks, and the sheep stumbled as they walked. In the desert, the men woke up to find scorpions crawling across their blankets, and sometimes they came across rattlesnakes. Still, they continued, hopeful that they would soon find the gleaming cities of Cibola. Each time they approached a village, Coronado sent a few men ahead. The men carried a large cross into the city, because many Native Americans recognized the cross as a symbol of peace. The men also carried beads and knives to give as gifts. After the gifts were given to the village leaders, Coronado and the rest of the group would then ride into the city.

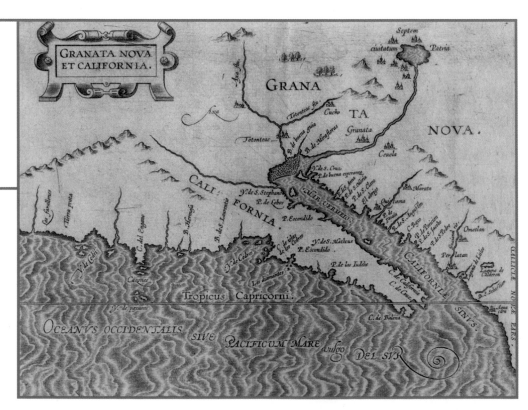

This map shows Cibola, where Coronado and his men first went to find gold.

*Corn Mountain overlooks the Zuni **pueblo** in northwestern New Mexico. The modern pueblo is built on the ruins of the one from Coronado's time, and it is still in use.*

Running out of supplies

As they traveled, Coronado wondered what had happened to the supply ships. Their food supply was dwindling, and his men were always hungry. By this time, he had expected to be met by a messenger from the ship with news of how to arrange to get the supplies. If they did not get more food soon, his men would starve.

One day Coronado's scouting party came across a river flowing with red, muddy water. They named it the Red River. Today, it is known as the Little Colorado River. As they rested there for a few days, Fray Marcos assured Coronado that they were getting closer to Cibola. Not long afterward, some men from Cibola came to their camp. Coronado gave them a large cross to take back to their village as a symbol of peace. He told the Cibolans that he and his men would soon visit their village.

Cibola

YOU CAN FOLLOW CORONADO'S EXPEDITION ON THE MAP ON PAGES 42–43.

Coronado sent a small group of men led by Garcia Lopez de Cardenas ahead to Cibola, while he and the rest of the men waited behind. The soldiers had expected to see tall buildings, lush gardens, and gold and silver. Instead, they found a small, crowded village—the **pueblo** of Hawikuh. The entire region was called Cibola, and the people who lived there are now known as the Zuni. The homes were in one large building made of stone and **adobe.**

Cardenas and his men cautiously approached the pueblo. They gave gifts to the people there and were pleased at how peaceful they seemed. That night, though, while the Spaniards slept at their camp outside the pueblo, some Zuni men attacked them. Cardenas sent a messenger back to Coronado, telling him that the Zuni people were ready to fight to defend Hawikuh.

Battle at Hawikuh

Coronado was disappointed when the messenger told him about "Cibola." It was not a great, shining city of gold—instead, it was a pueblo much like the others they had seen. But there would be food in the village, and his men were starving, so Coronado decided to go ahead and capture Hawikuh anyway.

As he and the other members of the scouting party approached, the Zuni warriors gathered. Coronado told them that they must turn over their city to him and obey his king. The Zuni refused,

Hundreds of years after Coronado's expedition, Mary Colter designed buildings for Grand Canyon National Park, using local stone. She was influenced by Native American building styles.

choosing to fight instead. But their rough weapons were little match against the steel swords of the Spaniards. It didn't take long for Coronado's men to overpower the Zuni and take control of Hawikuh.

During the battle, Coronado was hit on the head by a large stone thrown by the Zuni. He had to leave the battle and be taken to a tent, where he rested. After they captured Hawikuh, the Spaniards stormed the village, looking for food. They had a great feast and celebrated their victory, but they were still angry with Fray Marcos for misleading them. They began to wonder if their entire **expedition** would be a failure. If it was, they knew who to blame.

Fray Marcos left the expedition and returned to Mexico in shame. He settled in a small Mexican village, where he mostly kept to himself. His reputation was ruined.

In Coronado's words:

In a report he wrote to **Viceroy** Mendoza, Coronado described Cardenas's visit to Cibola:

" . . . he found two or three poor villages, with twenty or thirty huts apiece. From the people here he learned that there was nothing to be found in the country beyond except the mountains. . . . The whole company felt disturbed by this, that a thing so much praised, and about which the father [Fray Marcos] had said so many things, should be found so very different; and they began to think that all the rest would be of the same sort."

Scouting Parties

You can follow Coronado's expedition on the map on pages 42–43.

Coronado's army was discouraged. Would they ever find the Seven Cities of Gold? They began to doubt whether they should go on. But they trusted their leader. When he made the decision to continue exploring the region, they followed him. To make sure the **expedition** covered as much ground as it could in its search, Coronado sent out small scouting parties.

Finding the Hopi

One of these scouting parties was led by Captain Pedro de Tovar. His group of seventeen men, along with several Zuni guides, headed west on July 15, 1540, while Coronado and the main army headed east and north. Tovar and his men explored parts of Arizona and visited a Hopi Indian village. They quickly conquered the village. By the middle of August they had returned to the main army.

*Coronado and his men were impressed by the **pueblos** of the Native Americans. Many of them were several stories tall.*

Most of the world had never heard of the Grand Canyon when Cardenas and his small group of men explored it in 1540.

The Grand Canyon

Another group of 25 men, led by Garcia Lopez de Cardenas, left on August 25, 1540, and went into what is now northwestern Arizona. There they saw a spectacular sight—the Grand Canyon and the great Colorado River that flows through it. Some of the men tried to get to the river on horseback. They rode downward for a long time, but finally had to turn back when they realized how deep the canyon was. When they returned to Coronado's camp they told him of the magnificent canyon they had found. He was amazed by their story, but he was unhappy that they had still not found gold.

In Castaneda's words:

In his **memoirs** of his adventures with Coronado, Pedro de Castaneda tells how Melchior Diaz went with twenty-five men to look for the seacoast to find out what had happened to the supply ships. They found a **province** of people who were like giants. Historians believe that this tribe was the Cocoa. Castaneda describes them this way:

"... they came to a province of exceedingly tall and strong men—like giants. They are naked and live in straw cabins built underground like smoke-houses, with only the straw roof above ground. They enter these at one end and come out at the other. More than a hundred persons, old and young, sleep in one cabin. When they carry anything, they can take a load of more than three or four hundred weight on their heads."

Bigotes and El Turco

YOU CAN FOLLOW CORONADO'S EXPEDITION ON THE MAP ON PAGES 42–43.

Coronado stayed at Cibola for a while. There, a curious band of Pecos Indians came to visit them, including two chiefs. They lived in a village called Cicuye—now Pecos, New Mexico—and wanted to see the people who had conquered the Zuni. The Spaniards nicknamed one of the chiefs "Bigotes," which means "whiskers," because he had a long mustache. They called the other man Cacique. Bigotes told Coronado that the Spaniards would be welcome in their **pueblo.** Then the two leaders exchanged gifts. When Bigotes left on August 29, 1540, Coronado sent Captain Hernando de Alvarado and twenty other men to go back to Cicuye with him.

Tiguex

The Indians first led the Spaniards to a great pueblo called Acoma. It was the largest pueblo the Spaniards had ever seen. Then, on September 7, they went to a pleasant valley on the Rio Grande River. Alvarado sent a message back to Coronado that the valley would be a good place to camp for the winter. When he received the message, Coronado sent more soldiers to the area, called Tiguex after the Tigua natives who lived there, to set up a camp.

Coronado's army set up camp in a lush valley next to the Rio Grande.

El Turco

After sending his message to Coronado, Alvarado went with Bigotes to Cicuye. There he met a young man who said he had been kidnapped from his tribe—probably Pawnee—by Bigotes, and that he was forced to work as a slave in Cicuye. The Spaniards thought he looked like a Turk, so they called him "El Turco." Bigotes gave permission for El Turco and another slave to guide Alvarado and his men to see the strange "cattle" on the plains. These cattle were actually **bison.**

Like many other explorers of the time, Coronado often depended on Native American guides.

El Turco soon discovered that the men were looking for the cities of gold. He said that he knew of such a place, called Quivira, to the northeast. The people there rode in canoes decorated with gold, he said. Golden ornaments hung from the trees, and everyone—even servants—ate from golden plates and bowls. El Turco said he could prove that he had been to Quivira, because when he was kidnapped, he had two golden bracelets from there.

Alvarado returned to Cicuye and demanded to see the bracelets, but Bigotes and Cacique claimed that El Turco was lying. That night, Alvarado asked Bigotes and Cacique to visit him. When they came out of the pueblo, Alvarado had them put into chains. As soon as the men inside the pueblo discovered this, they came out to fight. They were angry with Alvarado for misusing his friendship with them. They said that there were no bracelets, and that El Turco was lying. As he watched, El Turco smiled. The story of the bracelets was a lie. He had told it because he wanted to get **revenge** on Bigotes for capturing him and making him a slave.

The Spaniards Attack

YOU CAN FOLLOW CORONADO'S EXPEDITION ON THE MAP ON PAGES 42–43.

Alvarado brought the prisoners back to Coronado's camp at Tiguex. Many of the Spaniards camped there were not happy to see the **hostages.** They felt that Alvarado had gone too far and that now the Native Americans would no longer trust a Spaniard's word. Then Coronado, worried about the coming winter, ordered soldiers to march to nearby **pueblos** and demand that the people give them warm blankets. This angered the Native Americans even more.

Coronado's men needed warm blankets to survive the winter. The Native Americans of the Southwest are still known for their beautifully patterned blankets.

Attack on Arenal

When Coronado discovered that some men from the pueblo of Arenal had stolen some of his mules, he ordered Cardenas to attack the pueblo. The Spaniards fought their way into the

In Castaneda's words:

"They all work together to build the villages, the women being engaged in making the mixture and the walls, while the men bring the wood and put it in place....they make a mixture of ashes, coals, and dirt which is almost as good as mortar, for when the house is to have four stories, they do not make the walls more than a half a yard thick. They gather a great pile of twigs and thyme and sedge grass and set it afire, and when it is half coals and ashes they throw a quantity of dirt and water on it and mix it all together. They make round balls of this, which they use instead of stones after they are dry, fixing them with the same mixture."

fortress and captured about 100 people. The people of Arenal made signs of surrender, and some of the Spaniards saw them. Cardenas, however, did not. He ordered his men to kill the hostages. A few escaped and spread the news throughout the region that the Spaniards had not kept their promise of peace and friendship, even when the people of Arenal had tried to surrender.

More attacks

Coronado then sent some of his captains, including Cardenas, to nearby villages, ordering them to surrender. At a village called Moho, the chief acted friendly to Cardenas. But when Cardenas came closer, two men attacked. The Spaniards and several of the Indians fought for a few minutes, and Cardenas was shot in the leg with an arrow. He rode back to Coronado and told him what had happened.

To show the power of his army, Coronado laid **siege** to Moho. The Tigua people stayed behind their walls and refused to come out. Finally, by March 1541, they had run out of water. They fled in the middle of the night, killing the Spaniards who were watching them. At least 100 of the fleeing Native Americans were killed. Then the Spaniards took the women and children from both villages as slaves. Before they left, the Spaniards set fire to the village.

The Spanish explorers were fascinated by the way the grass on the Great Plains sprang up behind them as they passed, making it look as if their army of more than 1,000 people had never passed through.

Searching for Quivira

You can follow Coronado's expedition on the map on pages 42–43.

By the spring of 1541, Coronado was ready to start searching for Quivira. He brought El Turco along to show him the way. On their way, the explorers stopped at Cicuye to return the **hostages.** There, El Turco had secret meetings with the Native American chiefs of Cicuye. The chiefs wanted to get **revenge** on Coronado and his men for kidnapping their leaders and for the battle at Moho. With El Turco they came up with a secret plan. Instead of leading the Spaniards to Quivira, El Turco would get them lost on the plains. He would make sure there was no food or water there, so that the Spaniards would eventually die.

In Coronado's words:

"And what I am sure of is that there is not any gold nor any other metal in all that country, and the other things of which they had told me are nothing but little villages, and in many of these they do not plant anything and do not have any houses except of skins and sticks, and they wander around with the cows . . ."

Coronado wrote this in a report to Mendoza about Quivira.

The Tejas

The **expedition** left for Quivira on April 23, 1541. On the way, they returned Bigotes and Cacique to their villages. After traveling a few days, the explorers came across a friendly tribe they called the Tejas,

The Tejas people were known for their skill at weaving baskets.

because the Native Americans said "Tejas" in greeting. The Tejas observed El Turco's behavior and listened to his stories of great riches in Quivira, then took some of the Spanish leaders aside and told them that El Turco was a liar.

At Quivira the Spaniards expected to see homes decorated with gold and silver. Instead, they saw grass huts similar to this one.

Hearing this, Coronado decided to take a small group to see if the Tejas were correct. He gathered 36 men, and they set off to search for the city while the rest of the expedition went back to Tiguex. El Turco went with Coronado, this time in chains. The small group traveled for more than 30 days. They went through parts of present-day Texas—named after the Tejas tribe—and parts of Oklahoma and Kansas.

Quivira

The travelers finally found Quivira at the end of June 1541. The Native Americans who lived there—probably Wichita—lived in grass huts. There was no gold or silver hanging from the trees. That night, El Turco finally admitted that he had been lying all along. To get free from slavery with Bigotes, he had made up a story he knew the Spaniards wanted to hear so they would take him along as their guide. Then he told them that he and the two chiefs had made up a plan to lead the Spaniards into the plains to die. Angry that he had been misled, Coronado ordered his men to kill El Turco.

Coronado claimed Quivira for Spain and forced the people there to pledge their loyalty to the Spanish king. The Spaniards spent a month in Quivira and at a nearby village, Haraya. Then the disappointed Spaniards rode back to Tiguex.

A Fall from a Horse

YOU CAN FOLLOW CORONADO'S EXPEDITION ON THE MAP ON PAGES 42–43.

Winter was coming, so Coronado decided that the **expedition** would stay at their camp at Tiguex until spring. While they waited, the men relaxed and played games. Sometimes they raced on horseback. Coronado and a friend had just such a race on December 27, 1541. As the horses galloped, the strap that held Coronado's saddle broke. The saddle slid sideways, and Coronado fell to the ground in front of Maldonado's horse. Before Maldonado could stop, his horse stepped on Coronado's head. Coronado was seriously injured and almost died.

The Tiwa **pueblo** of Kuaua, one of many visited by Coronado, is now part of the Coronado State Monument near Bernalillo, New Mexico.

In Castaneda's words:

As they journeyed through North America, the Spaniards were fascinated by **bison**, which then roamed the Southwest and plains in huge herds. Pedro de Castaneda described them this way:

"... they have a narrow, short face, the brow two palms across from eye to eye, the eyes sticking out at the side, so that, when they are running, they can see who is following them. They have very long beards, like goats, and when they are running they throw their heads back with the beard dragging on the ground. There is a sort of girdle round the middle of the body. The hair is very woolly, like a sheep's, very fine, and in front of the girdle the hair is very long and rough like a lion's. They have a great hump, larger than a camel's. The horns are short and thick, so that they are not seen much above the hair."

This woodcut of a bison, made in 1558, was probably drawn by someone who had never seen a real bison, just read descriptions of them.

End of the expedition

Although he eventually did recover, Coronado was never quite the same again. His men noticed the difference in him and did not obey him as well as they had before. The soldiers began to talk among themselves about whether they should keep searching for the cities of gold. They knew that before he fell, Coronado wanted to continue the search. But many of the soldiers were tired of searching for the cities and wanted to return home to New Spain. They wrote a letter requesting to return home, and everyone signed it. Then they gave the letter to Coronado. Later, some of the soldiers felt they had been tricked into signing the letter. They tried to get the letter back, but it was too late. Coronado told the army to prepare to return to New Spain.

Journey's End

You can follow Coronado's expedition on the map on pages 42–43.

In April 1542, the army left Tiguex. Two **friars,** Juan de Padilla and Friar Luis Descalona, stayed behind to **convert** the Native Americans. Padilla stayed at Quivira, and Descalona went to Cicuye. Not long afterward, Padilla was killed at Quivira.

During their **expedition,** Coronado and his men had captured Native Americans and kept them as servants. Before they departed Tiguex, Coronado told the prisoners that they were free to go. It is said that before he left, Coronado also had a large cross made and raised it near either Tiguex or Quivira. On the cross was written: "Thus far came Francisco de Coronado, General of the Expedition." The cross has never been found.

The army deserts

According to one story, on the return journey Coronado often had to be carried on a stretcher because he was still recovering from his head injury. As they neared Mexico, many of the soldiers dropped behind. They were worried about how the people of Mexico and **Viceroy** Mendoza would receive them. Their expedition was a failure—they had not found gold, nor had they discovered a water route to Asia. Now they had to face their families, friends, and leaders and tell them that they had failed.

Because they did not find gold or other treasures for Spain, Coronado and his men felt like failures when their journey ended.

When Coronado entered Mexico City, only about 100 soldiers were with him. Their clothes were in rags, and many of them had lice. Some of the horses had collapsed and died on the journey, and the surviving horses walked slowly. The huge army that had left New Spain full of hope was in tatters.

Many buildings from Coronado's time are still standing in Mexico City today.

Back in New Spain

Viceroy Mendoza was not pleased by the reports of the returning army. Coronado had sent him reports as he explored, so Mendoza knew that the expedition had not found what it had expected to. When he saw the men, Mendoza declared their expedition a failure.

Mendoza allowed Coronado to return as governor of New Galicia. Then the government put Coronado through an inspection, as they often did with leaders. They examined his leadership during the expedition and as governor. Some of the soldiers on the expedition had accused Coronado of being a poor leader and of mistreating Native Americans. He was cleared of all charges in connection with the expedition, but he was found guilty of mistreating natives and of **corruption** during his governorship. The title of general was taken away from him, and he was removed as governor. He moved to Mexico City, where he became a member of the city council. On September 22, 1554, Coronado died. He was buried in the cemetery at Santo Domingo Church in Mexico City.

Cabrillo explored southern California, including locations that are popular tourist spots today, such as San Diego and Catalina Island.

Cabrillo and Ferrer

While Coronado's army was still traveling, Mendoza sent out another **expedition** to explore the Pacific coast north of Mexico. The expedition, led by Juan Rodriguez Cabrillo, left Mexico in June 1542. Three small ships sailed up the coast of Baja California to southern California. Cabrillo stopped there to claim all the land for the king of Spain. Then the ships continued to sail up the coast.

They stopped at the harbors of San Diego, San Pedro, and Santa Barbara and mapped those areas. To wait out the winter, the expedition stopped at Santa Catalina Island. There, Cabrillo died, probably from complications after breaking his leg. Cabrillo's chief pilot, Bartoleme Ferrer, decided to continue the trip. Ferrer sailed north along the coast all the way to the Rogue River, which is in present-day Oregon.

Espejo and the priests

For many years after Coronado's expedition, Europeans did not explore southwestern North America. Because Coronado had found no silver or gold, the leaders of Spain saw no reason to spend money exploring the land further. But in 1581, three priests, along with a few Spanish soldiers, traveled from Mexico into New Mexico. They stayed with a Native American tribe, hoping to **convert** them to Christianity. The soldiers returned to Mexico.

*Visited by both Coronado and Oñate, the **pueblo** of Acoma is considered to be the oldest continuously inhabited city in the United States.*

In 1582, Antonio de Espejo, along with Father Beltran and fourteen soldiers, left Mexico to look for the priests. They discovered that all three priests had been killed. While speaking with the Native Americans, Espejo was surprised to meet three Mexican men. They said that they had been with Coronado's expedition and had stayed behind to live with the natives. Espejo then returned to Mexico.

Oñate

In 1598, **Don** Juan de Oñate got permission from Spain to secure the border of New Spain. Oñate was also ordered to spread the Catholic faith to the people in the north. He led his expedition north, taking possession of every town he saw. He also thought he might find the wealthy cities that Coronado had failed to locate. Then Oñate's nephew, following behind his uncle, offended the people of Acoma, which Coronado's men had visited earlier. The nephew and other Spaniards were killed, and Oñate came to Acoma and waged a great battle, killing more than 800 Native Americans. Many others were taken as slaves. The Acoma village was later rebuilt, but it was never the same.

Coronado's Legacy

While Coronado's **expedition** did not achieve its goal of finding the Seven Cities of Gold, it actually contributed a great deal—both good and bad—to Europe and North America. The people of Coronado's expedition were the first Europeans to meet and talk with many Native American tribes in the Southwest. They were the first to see and describe North American wildlife, such as **bison** and Rocky Mountain sheep. They found out how Native Americans used bison skins to make clothing and parts of their homes, and how they prepared bison meat. The Coronado expedition also discovered that the **prickly pear** could be a valuable food when traveling in the desert.

Geography

In the two years the expedition traveled, it covered a large area of what is now the United States. Members of Coronado's army traveled through arid deserts, up high mountains, and across vast plains. One group, led by Cardenas, found and described the Grand Canyon. For a time they followed the Colorado,

The modern city of Coronado, California, on the tip of a peninsula near San Diego, is now a popular tourist destination.

Kansas, Arkansas, and Rio Grande rivers. The expedition covered more land than any other European expedition up to that time. From the reports of their travels, mapmakers in Europe were able to map more of the North American continent.

This statue and a museum containing items from Coronado's time are in Liberal, Kansas. Coronado stopped near Liberal while he was searching for Quivira.

Horses

The Spaniards contributed to Native Americans a very important animal—the horse. Before Coronado's expedition, there were no horses north of Mexico. When Native Americas saw the Spaniards sitting atop these animals, they were at first frightened. Some even spread the rumor that horses would eat people. During Coronado's expedition, some of the horses were stolen by Native Americans, and others ran off. Soon the Native Americans began using horses themselves. With them, they were able to ride farther and faster from one place to another. **Bison** hunts were safer, because the hunters could move around more quickly in bison herds. Horses became a very important article of trade among Native Americans.

Disease

Another legacy the Spanish explorers left behind was disease, when they exposed the people of North America to germs from Europe. The people of Europe had been exposed to the germs for years, and they had built up **immunity** to them. But the Native Americans did not have immunity to European diseases, and thousands of people in New Spain and the rest of North America died from these new diseases.

Map of Coronado's Expedition

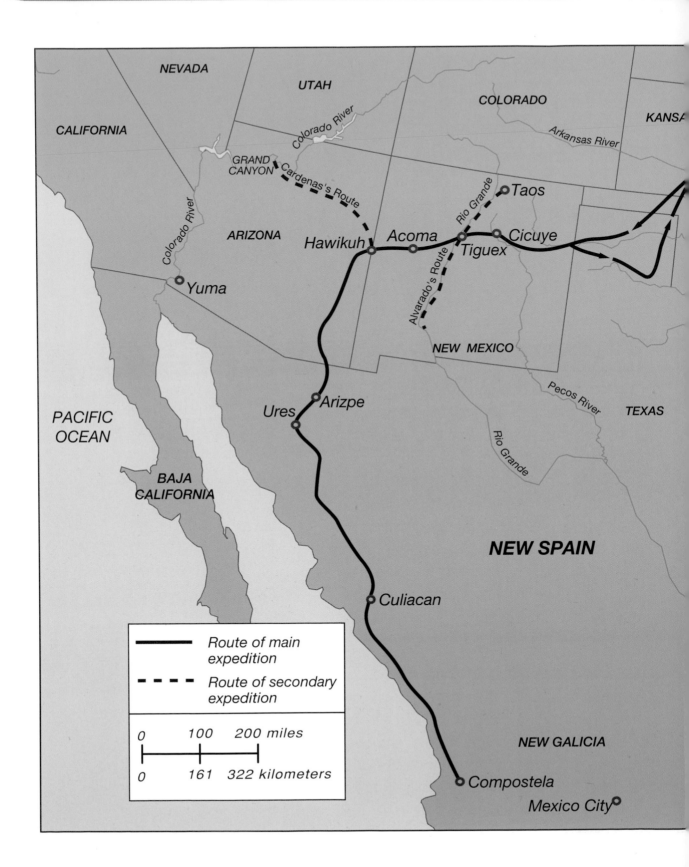

NEVADA

UTAH

COLORADO

KANSAS

CALIFORNIA

Colorado River

Arkansas River

GRAND CANYON

Cardenas's Route

Taos

Rio Grande

Colorado River

ARIZONA

Hawikuh

Acoma

Cicuye

Tiguex

Alvarado's Route

Yuma

NEW MEXICO

PACIFIC OCEAN

Arizpe

Ures

Pecos River

TEXAS

Rio Grande

BAJA CALIFORNIA

NEW SPAIN

Culiacan

	Route of main expedition
- - -	Route of secondary expedition

0   100   200 miles

0   161   322 kilometers

NEW GALICIA

Compostela

Mexico City

Timeline

1492   Christopher Columbus discovers islands of the New World in the Caribbean Sea.

1496   John and Sebastian Cabot reach the east coast of North America.

1500   Pedro Alvares Cabral discovers Brazil and claims it for Portugal.

1502   Amerigo Vespucci determines that South America is a continent separate from India.

1506   Christopher Columbus dies.

1510?   Francisco Vásquez de Coronado is born.

1513   Juan Ponce de Leon discovers Florida.

1518   Juan de Grijalva discovers Mexico.

1519   Cortés enters Mexico, eventually conquering it and claiming it for Spain. Ferdinand Magellan leaves Europe to sail around the world.

1521   Magellan is killed by natives in the Philippines.

1522   Pascual de Andagoya leads a land **expedition** from Panama and discovers Peru.

1524   Giovanni de Verrazano discovers New York Bay.

1527   Panfilo de Narvaez leads an expedition to colonize Florida.

1530   Portugal sets up **colonies** in Brazil.

1535   Coronado accompanies Antonio de Mendoza to Mexico.

1536   Survivors of Narvaez's expedition, including Estevanico, arrive in Mexico.

1538   Coronado becomes governor of New Galicia and marries Beatriz Estrada.

1539   In March, Fray Marcos and Estevanico leave to find the cities of gold. Fray Marco returns in September, saying that he saw the great city of Cibola.

         Hernando de Soto explores Florida.

1540	Coronado's expedition to find the Seven Cities of Gold begins on February 22.
1541	Coronado, following El Turco's directions, leads his men to find the great city of Quivira (August 23). Coronado falls from his horse and is seriously injured (December 27).
	Hernando de Soto discovers the Mississippi River.
1542	Coronado's expedition returns to New Spain.
	Hernando de Soto dies.
1544	Coronado is accused of being a poor leader and of treating the Native Americans cruelly. As punishment, some of his personal property is taken from him.
1546	Coronado is cleared of the charges.
1552	Antonio de Mendoza dies.
1554	Coronado dies on September 22.
1565	Pedro de Castaneda writes and publishes an account of the Coronado expedition, called *The Narrative of the Expedition of Coronado*.

More Books to Read

Favor, Lesli J. *Francisco Vasquez de Coronado: Famous Journeys to the American Southwest*. New York: Rosen Publishing Group, Inc., 2002.

January, Brendan. *Hernán Cortés*. Chicago: Heinemann Library, 2003.

Nardo, Don. *Francisco Coronado*. Danbury, Conn.: Franklin Watts, 2001.

Glossary

adobe brick made of dried mud, used for building

astronomy study of objects in the sky, such as stars

Aztec people who founded an empire in Mexico, conquered by Cortés in 1519

bison large, shaggy animal that is related to the cow. It is often called "buffalo," but scientists do not consider it a true buffalo.

caravan group of vehicles traveling together

colony group of people sent out by a state or country to settle a new territory

conquistador leader in the Spanish conquest of the Americas in the fifteenth and sixteenth centuries

convert to persuade someone to change their religious beliefs, either by choice or by force

corruption lack of honesty

court king or queen and his or her circle of councilors, advisers, friends, and relatives

dike high bank built to stop the flow of water

Don Spanish title of respect, similar to "Sir"

ducat gold coin formerly used in many parts of Europe

empire group of territories or peoples under one ruler

estate entire property that someone leaves at death

expedition trip taken to discover new places

friar member of some Roman Catholic religious groups. Friars are not priests; they often work in hospitals or schools.

gully trench worn in the earth by running water

hostage someone held prisoner to make sure that promises will be kept

immunity ability to fight off disease

inherit to get by legal right from a person after their death

lance weapon with a long handle and a sharp steel head

memoirs report of a personal experience, usually written in story form

merchant someone who buys and sells goods

noble belonging to a class of people with certain social privileges and high social standing

philosophy study of the basic ideas about knowledge, right and wrong, reasoning, and the value of things

plague disease that spreads and infects many people

plaza public square in a city or town

prickly pear sweet, pear-shaped fruit that grows on a spiny cactus with flat branching joints

privilege right granted as a favor to some people but not others

province part of a country having a government of its own

pueblo Native American village in the southwestern United States, made up of groups of stone or adobe houses with flat roofs

rebellion open fight by people against their government

revenge harm or injury caused to someone in return for their actions

siege surrounding of a fortified place, usually for a long time, in order to capture it

treasury department of a government that deals with money and taxes

university institution of higher learning that gives degrees in special fields

viceroy leader of a country or province who rules as the representative of a king of queen

wrangler person who takes care of horses

Index